<= The Far Corners

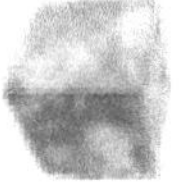

of the Globe=>

====> More off-center

poetry by

Michael Lowe Wright <==

*For all those who have suffered from,
and those who have lost their lives to,
Covid19 and Long Covid
in this disastrous pandemic.
Many of these poems were written
while I was in its clutches.*

*If life's only an illusion
What's really going on...*

Table of Contents

A Soleless Shoe

A soleless shoe*
Adorns an orphanage
It is good
To inspire the young
To aspire to
The great deeds
Of their heritage
To dream
And scheme
To go through life
Alert to opportunity
Primed for action
And always wearing
The right shoes

1/30/2009

*A monument, 8.2 "feet" long, 4.9 feet wide, and 11.5 feet high, in the image of a giant copper shoe on a concrete pedestal, was built at an Iraqi orphange in honor of Muntadhir al-Zaidi. It was al-Zaidi who threw his shoes at then-President George W. Bush, who was giving a press conference while on a visit to Baghdad in December of 2008. Such an act is considered the highest form of insult in the Arab world, and al-Zaidi is viewed as a hero by many Iraqis.

The Sun's Stony Pyre

The Sun's Stony Pyre
Squats
Looms
Invites
I rise
To the challenge
Else
I'll never know what
The Ancients saw up there
Building this
Wasn't a weekend backyard project
They were after something
As I climb the 248 steps
My mind rises too
I'm taken back to times unknown
A stranger
In a mysterious land
Below...
The Avenue of the Dead
...Is alive
At last
I reach the summit
Ready to inhale
Inspiration of things past
Instead I find
A muchacho hawking popsicles
A tourist with a camera
Its lens
Hanging down his chest
Like a monstrous
Limp penis
--

In that moment
My understanding
Of the roots and causes
Of human sacrifice
Took a whole new turn

3/29/2022

In the Quiet Times

In the quiet times
I seek solace
From a world that's
Jumped the shark
Vicariously
Slay a few vampires
Defeat terrorism
Win the war
Then
The screen goes black
My mind returns
To now
Where evil runs rampant
And I'm no hero
Trying to survive
The madness
That seems to have
No end

4/18/2022

The Ultimate World Traveler

The ultimate world traveler
Hopped a ride
In a wet market
And was off
Touring the far corners
Of the globe
Invisible
Spoiler of lives
Murderer of millions
Unstopped
Unstoppable
Does a raucous
Viral laugh echo
As it mows down
The arrogant
And
The humble
Alike?

4/19/2022

The Sun Rises On Another Day

The Sun rises on another day
Its rays fall
Without care or favor
Long had they lit the stage when
Strutting and fretting arose
And will, still, when the set
Has long been struck
The idiot's fury dissipated
And the players' dust
Swept clean away

4/21/2022

He Really Had A Way

He really had a way
With words
You never saw him without
A couple of them
Vying for his attention
He'd go down to
The Dictionary
And leave with
A whole herd
Nouns, verbs, adjectives
They all adored him
And jumped to do
His bidding
It wasn't all sweetness
And light though
The ones inflated with
Their own popularity
Would sometimes
Leave in a huff
--
He liked his words
Like he liked his liquor
Humble
Straightforward
Nuanced
And comfortable with
Carrying his meaning

4/23/2022

We Do Not Live Under

We do not live under
The dome of the sky
That is an illusion
We live in the sky
Lost in a foggy cloud
Blued by distance
How can we think
We are separate?
There is no boundary
No veil to be pierced
No place at which
It stops being there
And becomes here
The Sun... the Moon
The stars and planets
The galaxies and nebulas
They all live here too
Nearer to our eyes
Than even the closest
Corner of the globe
Which lies hidden
Behind the horizon
Sky's ancient enemy
And the only fence
Able to confine it

4/26/2022

From a Scrap of Paper

From a scrap of paper
Found
After a thunderstorm:
--
At last
After many days' travel
We draw near to
The end of the rainbow
An inaudible hum
Infuses the air
All vibrancy
Is drained
From the landscape
Fearsome fields
Of extracted color
Swirl
Into its maelstrom
We must return
And report
That there is no gold
But
We find ourselves
Mesmerized
Bewar
--
That is all
It said

4/29/2022

O Wakulla

O Wakulla
Mightiest of springs
Gathered
From her veins
Sheltered
And purified
You erupt from
The Earth Mother
Relentlessly reborn
A mother yourself
Multitudes
Carrying you
In their veins
You give the gift
Of life
Nourishing
Sustaining
Asking nothing
In return
Only that we
Respect and protect
As any dutiful child
Must
We praise
Your bounty and
Your beauty
Though we will pass
May you always
Bless this place
And all who
Come after us

4/30/2022

In a Capital Somewhere

In a capital somewhere
Weapons roll
Martial music
Blares
Crescendos
Fades into
Echoes
Crowds cheer
The Leader speaks
Of enemies
And glory
Of victories past
And to come
Or at least
Hoped for
Again and again
Evil is defeated
Yet is it not
Evil
Who even now
Speaks
--
All is
Echoes

5/9/2022

The Phoenix Stands

The Phoenix stands
Among the ashes
Reborn from fire
Hatched from
Its own egg
Much has it seen
Much forgotten
All burned away
Cleansed
As ever has it been
But this time
Is different
This time
It will not be bound
By what has been before
Tangled
In its own legend
Doomed always to
Crash and burn
Not again
This time
It will create
Its own fate
Its heart soars
It spreads its wings
Flies away
Into the red and golden
Dawn

5/14/2022

I Sit in the Moonlight

I sit in the moonlight
Some trees stand proudly
Others bow humbly
All join with the moon
To cast a net of shadows
Mingling into one
Mirroring the roots
That join them below
A distant storm pulses
With its lightning heartbeart
Its churning masses
Lit from within
There is no clever obfuscation
No veiled meanings
It all speaks directly to my soul
It is not to blame
If I do not understand

5/15/2022

You Have Discovered Nothing

You have discovered nothing
You left the land
Of your birth
Dark
Filled with knowledge
Of life and beyond
You return
Bleached
Empty of heart and head
Your soul shriveled
You think you have
Discovered
What was here all along
As much as we may
We will drive you
From among us
Perhaps you will return
Overpower us
With your numbers
Rot us with your poison
Destroy our lands
As you have destroyed
Your own
But even in your
Hollow victory
Still you will have
Discovered nothing
Except your own arrogance

5/15/2022

The Crow Cawcus Is Meeting

The crow cawcus is meeting
In the pine tree
Outside my window
Laughing down at us
Stuck on the ground
They strut from limb to limb
Cracking crow jokes like peanuts
They can laugh all they want
The joke's on them
Little do they know
They're in my poem

5/19/2022

In the Deep of Night

In the deep of night
Something flies
Across the blood-red face
Of the late-rising moon
A thing scarcely seen
A thing I wish I hadn't
The hair on my neck
Rises in chill salute
To a presence
That I sense
Growing ever closer
Invisible tendrils
Brush against my skin
I scream

5/19/2022

Rain Runs Down

Rain runs down
The window screen
Earth weeps for
Her wayward children
Though they wound her
Still she shelters them
Blesses them
With healing tears
They forgot
Their love for her
Became infatuated
With themselves
With their transient
Glory
All
Will return to dust
Magnificent temples
To rubble
Earth mourns
What might have been
And makes way
For what
Is to come

5/26/2022

In a Time Unmeasured

In a time unmeasured
In a place uncharted
The player sends breath
Awakens the Yidaki
And dissolves the veil
Between the worlds
Those who have been
And those yet to be
Join in the song
The Dreaming merges
Into the now
Duration merges
Into distance
All is one
Then the song
Circles back
To the beginning
All is harmonized
The universe's
Cycle complete
Order rearises
The whole splits again
Into its parts
The player dismisses them
Puts down the Yidaki
Time resumes
The stars safely
In their orbits
Once again

5/28/2022

One Summer Evening

One Summer evening
As I wandered the
Dark and winding byways
Of Choccolocco
A stationary cloud
Over a nearby peak
Revealed itself
Illumined from within
Dusky flashes
Like a primeval
Morse code
Long it sat there
Mystifying any who
Raised their eyes
To its level
What Moses stood
Atop that peak
What commandments
Did he receive
What God
Handed them down
Or were they meant
Solely for me
Living wordless
In my being
Until someone would
Listen to my tale
Understand
That magic and spirit
Still live
Still speak to us
If
We will but listen

5/29/2022

Hot Summer Day

Hot Summer day
Alabama 1964
Country store
Soft drinks captive in rigid rows
RC, Lotta Cola, Yoohoo!, Orange Crush
Some strawberry thing or other
Up to their necks in frigid water
I play Tower of Hanoi
To get that Choc Cola
At the end of a row
A dime opens the gate
I lift it dripping
Lever off the top in the opener
Mounted on the side of the box
It clatters into the pile
Of its discarded brethren
At the bottom
Fetch an ice cream sandwich
From the freezer
Back in the car
James Brown on the radio
--
Life is good

6/1/2022

If You Stand on Your Head

If you stand on your head
You can see the hidden stars
The birds who fly through water
The ever circling mountains of ice
Maybe you'll realize that
The Earth has no top or bottom
That gravity is
The father of down
That wherever you go
You are your own singularity
And everywhere else is up

6/4/2022

I Went To Visit Mother Ocean

I went to visit Mother Ocean
Immersed my feet and hands
In her body
She
And all who feed her
Are one
In that instant
I touched
All the rivers and oceans
Of the world
Melting snow
On the flanks
Of Chomolungma
The lake called
Kitchi-gami
The unnamed waters
Beneath the Earth
She called
To remind me
That I am borrowed water
That she lives in me
Flows through me
Walks on my feet
Over dry land
Rising above
Gravity's imperative
Before leaving my body
And merging back
Into herself

6/5/2022

I Live Near a Nest of Dragons

I live near a nest of dragons
They come and go at all hours
Roaring through the skies
Snagging my consciousness
Like a precious stone
Dragging it after them
Even unto
The far corners of the globe
Tame dragons they are
Yet sometimes they
Turn on their masters
Destroy themselves
And their puny riders
In consuming flame
Or plummet into
The unyielding Earth
The dead may disagree
But for the travel-hungry living
It's just the price
They must pay
For living with dragons

6/6/2022

Acknowledgements

*Long Covid for laying me low and
and forcing me onto the
kindness of strangers*

*Those strangers, found on Twitter, who
showed me exceptional kindness and
got me through one of the worst
times of my life*

*Jo of the Phoenix Book Cafe for support
and encouragement of my new passion for
writing poetry*

*Rob Arnol for insight into Aboriginal
culture and traditions*

About the Author

Had a fairly interesting life, did some stuff, went
some cool places, made some things, and now I'm old.
Funny how that works...

If you want the full bio, it's in my first book,
The Far Corner of the Room.

Or, you can just go with this:
I am the Wader in Deep Waters
I am the Stalking Heron
I am He Who Soars with Crows
He who Overtook the Roadrunner
I am Woods Walker
Herder of Words
Melder of Melodies
Prober of Mysteries
Wrangler of Algorithms
and
Servant of Euterpe

I currently reside at an undisclosed location
somewhere near Tallahassee, Florida.